ASTROLOGY

TAURUS

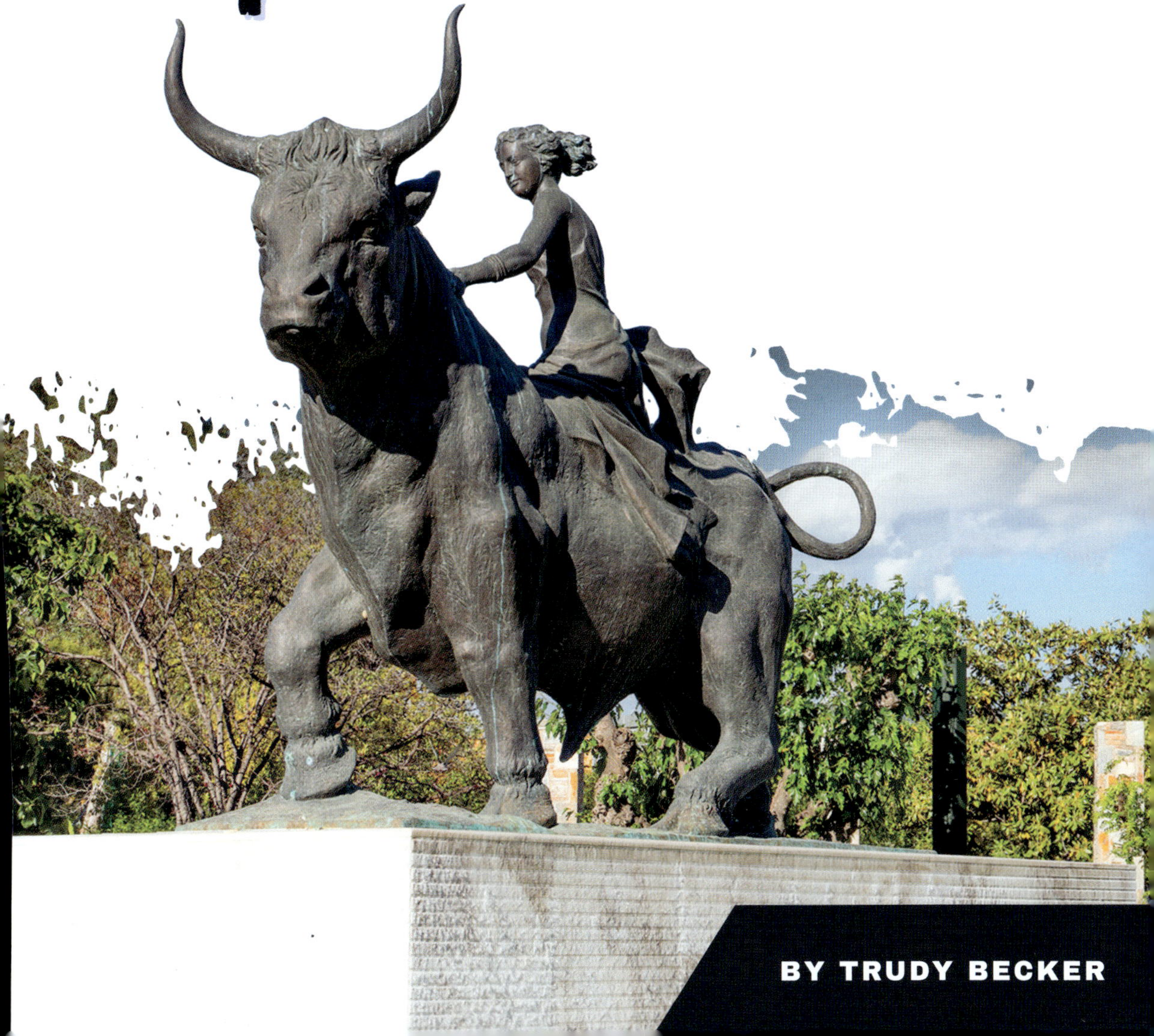

BY TRUDY BECKER

WWW.APEXEDITIONS.COM

Apex is distributed by North Star Editions:
sales@northstareditions.com | 888-417-0195

Produced for Apex by Red Line Editorial.

Photographs ©: Shutterstock Images, cover (illustration, constellation), cover (background), 1, 4–5, 6, 8, 9, 10–11, 12–13, 14, 18–19, 20, 21, 22–23, 24–25, 27, 29; Raphael Gaillarde/Gamma-Rapho/Getty Images, 7; iStockphoto, 16–17

Library of Congress Control Number: 2025939156

ISBN
979-8-89250-790-5 (hardcover)
979-8-89250-819-3 (paperback)
979-8-89250-876-6 (ebook pdf)
979-8-89250-848-3 (hosted ebook)

Printed in the United States of America
Mankato, MN
012026

TABLE OF CONTENTS

CHAPTER 1

A BULL IN THE SKY

Taurus is a **constellation**. Its main stars form two V shapes. The shapes connect in the middle.

TAURUS

In the night sky, Taurus is near the Hyades and Pleiades. Those are groups of stars.

Taurus was one of the first constellations that people identified. People thought the stars looked like a bull. They told stories about it. In ancient Greece, people linked it with the god Zeus.

In one story, the Greek god Zeus turned into a bull.

Very old paintings cover the walls of the Lascaux cave in France. Some of the paintings show bulls.

ANCIENT ART

Researchers think a cave painting from 15,000 BCE shows Taurus. It may include the Pleiades, too. That is a group of stars near the bull's shoulder.

The people of Sumer created one of the earliest writing systems.

Another tale came from Sumer. A goddess sent a monster called the Bull of Heaven to fight a king named Gilgamesh. The king's friend helped him kill it and throw parts of it into the sky.

Gilgamesh was a hero in ancient stories. He won many battles.

FAST FACT

Taurus means "bull" in Latin.

CHAPTER 2

TAURUS'S TIME

Taurus is the second sign of the **zodiac**. The zodiac splits the year into 12 parts. Each part lasts around 30 days.

Each of the 12 zodiac signs is matched with a different constellation. It shows a person, object, or animal.

Taurus's time goes from about April 20 to about May 20. People born during this time have Taurus as their **sun sign**. They are called Taureans.

In astrology, Taurus is one of three signs matched with spring. It comes between Aries and Gemini.

FIXED SIGNS

Taurus is a fixed sign. That means it comes in the middle of a season. In astrology, fixed signs are linked with plans and **routines**. People with these signs often want to keep things calm.

Astrology claims that signs shape how people think and act. For example, it says Taureans tend not to rush or worry.

FAST FACT

Taureans may move slowly. But that doesn't mean they're lazy. They just like to enjoy things.

Taureans tend to dislike being busy. They would rather relax.

CHAPTER 3

ABOUT TAURUS

The **glyph** for Taurus looks like a bull. A circle at the bottom is the bull's head. A curved line on top forms the horns.

Every zodiac sign has its own glyph.

Taureans are known for being down-to-earth. They say what they mean and focus on practical tasks.

Taurus is linked with the **element** earth. Earth signs are said to be grounded. They are good at staying calm and doing what needs to be done.

FAST FACT

Many Taureans enjoy spending time in nature.

Taurus's ruling planet is Venus. Astrology says ruling planets shape how people act. Venus has ties to beauty and the senses. And Taureans may seek things that look, smell, and feel good.

The planet Venus is named after the Roman goddess of love and beauty.

Many Taureans love fancy foods, especially desserts.

LIKING NICE THINGS

Many Taureans love things that feel comfortable or fancy. They may look at beautiful art. They may buy **luxury** items. And they may eat delicious food.

CHAPTER 4

A STEADY SIGN

Taureans are known for being hard workers. They want to do a good job. And they rarely give up.

Taureans often work hard to complete tasks or solve problems.

Taureans tend to know what they want and what they like. They do not change their minds easily. So, they can sometimes be **stubborn**.

FACING CHANGE

Taureans tend to like traditions and comfort. They often resist change. However, learning to be okay with change is important. It helps people continue to learn and grow.

Bulls are known for being strong. And Taureans can have strong opinions.

Taureans can be patient and dependable, too. They work hard to help their friends and family. And they do what they promise. People can count on them to finish what they start.

FAST FACT

Famous Taureans include Sabrina Carpenter, John Cena, and Angel Reese.

Taureans often help others. For example, they may help pack when a friend moves.

COMPREHENSION QUESTIONS

Write your answers on a separate piece of paper.

1. Write a few sentences describing the main ideas of Chapter 4.
2. Do you change your mind often? Why or why not?
3. What is the name for a sign that comes in the middle of a season?
    - A. a sun sign
    - B. a fixed sign
    - C. an earth sign
4. Why can change be hard for Taureans?
    - A. Change can involve lots of planning.
    - B. Change can end routines that they like.
    - C. Change tends to happen slowly.

5. What does **identified** mean in this book?

Taurus was one of the first constellations that people ***identified****. People thought the stars looked like a bull.*

A. found
B. lost
C. changed

6. What does **grounded** mean in this book?

Earth signs are said to be ***grounded****. They are good at staying calm and doing what needs to be done.*

A. stable and steady
B. bad at planning
C. easy to upset

Answer key on page 32.

GLOSSARY

constellation

A group of stars that form a shape.

element

One of four forces (air, earth, fire, or water) that each zodiac sign is matched with and said to be shaped by.

glyph

A shape that stands for a word or idea.

luxury

Of very high quality and often costing a lot.

routines

Sets of actions done regularly and in a certain order.

stubborn

Not willing to change how one thinks or acts.

sun sign

A person's main zodiac sign, which is decided by the date they were born.

zodiac

The set of 12 signs used in astrology, based on a part of the sky that the sun appears to move through each year.

TO LEARN MORE

BOOKS

Goldstein, Margaret J. *Mysteries of Stars*. Lerner Publications, 2021.

Ha, Christine. *Zeus*. Apex Editions, 2022.

McMullen, Gemma. *The Stars*. Little Blue House, 2025.

ONLINE RESOURCES

Visit **www.apexeditions.com** to find links and resources related to this title.

ABOUT THE AUTHOR

Trudy Becker lives in Minneapolis, Minnesota. She likes exploring new places and loves anything involving books.

INDEX

ANSWER KEY:
1. Answers will vary; 2. Answers will vary; 3. B; 4. B; 5. A; 6. A